MALLORCA

Editorial Escudo de Oro, S.A.

View of the cathedral and, on the left, the Lonja (Exchange).

Cathedral: the rose window in the presbytery, one of the largest in the world. ▷

THE ISLAND OF MAJORCA

It is the largest island in the Balearic archipelago, with a surface area of 3,640 km² and 320 km of coastline dotted with beautiful bays and coves and magnificent, white sandy beaches. It currently has a population of around 600,000 inhabitants.

In Roman times, Majorca was known as ''*Balearis Major*''. The origins of the earliest Majorcans are not absolutely certain, but it appears that the island was first inhabited at the beginning of the the

Bronze Age. Many centuries before the Christian Era, the first inhabitants of the island erected megalithic monuments, chiefly for burial purposes, known as *talaiots, taules* and *navetes* or *galeres*

Majorca's enviable situation in the Mediterranean led to colonisers and sailors fighting for possession of the island in ancient and medieval times. The Carthaginians invaded the island and used the native inhabitants *baliares* (a name which derives from their skill in using the sling) to swell the ranks of the punic armies. Majorca was con-

◁ *View of the cathedral presbytery.*

Partial view of Palma: the cathedral, the Almudaina Palace, the S'Hort del Rei Gardens and the Parque del Mar.

quered by the Romans in the 2nd century B.C. — although not without taking a beating from islanders for some time — and founded the city of Palma, which they made into the political, social and commercial centre of the Balearic archipelago. In 468 A.D. the Vandals overran the island and in the middle of the 6th century Majorca became part of the Byzantine Empire.

At the end of the 8th century, Majorca was taken by the Arabs who placed the Balearic archipelago under the sovereignty of the Caliphate of Cordova and gave Palma the name al-Madina-Mayurqa.

The island's history throughout the Middle Ages was turbulent. It was a fief of the "taifa" (small Arab kingdom) of Denia and, at the beginning of the 13th century, was overrun by the Almohades who laid waste the city of Palma and other Majorcan towns.

Under Arab rule, the island enjoyed a long period of splendour, only slightly marred by the constant onslaught of pirate attacks.

James I the Conqueror made

The Almudaina Palace and the S'Hort del Rei Gardens.

several vain attempts to take possession of the island until finally, in 1229, he succeeded in conquering it and making it, together with Roussillon and Montpellier, an independent kingdom. After the death of James I, his son of the same name became the first king of Majorca. However, after the islands were annexed to the Crown of Aragon by Peter IV, the history of Majorca followed the same course as that of Catalonia.

Now, the Balearic Islands constitute an autonomous region boasting Palma as its capital.

The Monument to Ramón Llull.

View of one of the three rooms in the Moorish baths.

The Almudaina Arch, ancient gateway into the walled city.

Entrance courtyard to the Oleza House.

The varied beauty of the Majorcan landscape, added to the unique charm of its many magnificent beaches, its mild climate, fascinating folklore and the hospitality of its people, has made the island a true tourists' paradise.

THE CITY OF PALMA

Palma, the capital of the archipelago, is one of the universally best-known tourist centres.

The island is linked to the peninsula by several sea-ferry services and by air, from the airport at Son Sant Joan, which handles flights to and from the world's major airports.

The charm of this city — ''the golden city'' as Rubén Darío called it in one of his poems — ranges from the peerless blue of the sea to the motley Paseo del Born or the elegant Paseo de Sagrera with all its extraordinary wealth of monuments.

The *Cathedral* rises above the ancient city wall which, until recent years, was on the very edge of the sea, giving the overall effect of a strange and beautiful stone ship. It is on the site of the ancient mosque, and the bell tower was begun during the reign of James I the Conqueror. Building of the Cathedral as such began in the 14th century and, up to its completion in the 17th century, was supervised by various architects, including Guillem Sagrera. This century, major reforms were carried out inside the Cathedral by the architect Antonio Gaudí.

The church covers an area of 7,000 m². It comprises a nave and two simple, parallel aisles. The centre nave, supported by 14 graceful columns, is 44 m high, 109.5 m long and 55 m wide. This imposing nave was built between the 14th and 17th centuries. The Cathedral as a whole brings together various architectural styles, but the overall unifying style is Gothic. The main front, which boasts a large rose-window over a 16th century doorway, was rebuilt last century. On the exterior, its most remarkable features are the 14th-century Gothic Almoina (Alms) doorway, the majestic square tower and the Gothic Mirador (Belvedere) doorway,

The popular giants in the Town Hall, known as "Els Gegants de la Sala".

Church of San Francisco.

which was the work of Guillem Sagrera, Pedro Morey and other artists.

In 1903, the architect Gaudí moved the choir, which was formerly in the middle of the church, to the Royal Chapel. The church is fascinating because of its luminosity, the gracefulness of its spaces and the formal balance of its majestic nave and aisles. Equally remarkable are the presbytery rose-window, which is among the largest in the world, and several stained-glass windows which illuminate the interior. This comprises the Royal Chapel, the Chapel of the Holy Trinity (which houses the tombs of James II and James III, and were the work of the sculptor Frederic Marés, and also the Gothic panel of Saint Eulalia), the Gothic tomb of Ramon Torrelles, the Gothic tombstone by Juan Font, the Plateresque tomb of Bishop Arnau de Mari, the tomb of Bishop Galiana and a valuable 18th-century altar-piece, the two latter being found in the Chapel of our Lady of the Crown.

Cloister of the Church of San Francisco.

Interior of the Maritime Museum.

Front of the Lonja. ▷

In addition, there is a very interesting museum of religious *objets d'art*.

The Almudaina Palace stands opposite the Cathedral, commanding a fine view of the bay of Palma. Once the royal palace of the kings of Majorca, and formerly an Arab fortress, James II made the Almudaina Palace his Royal Military Headquarters.

It consists of a series of buildings occupying an area of approximately 20,000 m². The enclosure is surrounded by sturdy walls and turrets. The Almudiana Palace, together with its immediate surroundings, forms part of the nucleus of the original city of Palma.

The four parapeted towers, the portico, the Gothic gallery and some windows with Romanesque remains are in a good state of conservation.

Inside the palace, and worthy of

The gardens around the Almudaina
Palace.

special note, are the beautiful
chapel of Saint Anne, completed in
1310 and with additions made at
the end of the 15th century by
Joan Sagrera. The area occupied
by the gardens of S'Hort del Rei,
the old palace kitchen gardens, has
undergone many changes, but is
currently to be seen restored once
more to its former lushness. S'Hort
del Rei stretches down from the
city wall, bordering on a modern
park called "Parque de Mar".
Between the 15th and 18th centuries, the inhabitants of Palma
built many fine examples of

View of the Rambla.

One of the windmills of El Jonquet.

domestic architecture in the form of *stately homes*: the Berga Palace, which now houses the Law Courts, the Gothic Oleo Mansion, the Palace of the Marquis of Palmer with its Renaissance façade, the Palace of the Marquis of Vivot, together with the Solleric Palace and the Oleza mansion, which is regarded as one of the most important of its kind.

Palma's *City Hall*, located in the Plaza de Cort, has an elegantly pro-

View of the city of Palma.

Partial view of the Paseo Marítimo, with the west dock and the Club de Mar.

portioned façade. It is a fascinating example of Renaissance style, including some Baroque features. The old clock on the façade — popularly known as En Figuera — contributes to the unmistakable character of this building which was begun at the end of the 16th century.

Of historical interest inside the City Hall is the dais, now reconstructed and housed on the ground floor of the building, from which proclamations were made. The City Hall also houses a public library.

On the site of the old convent of Saint Dominic was built the "Círculo Mallorquín" (Majorcan Circle), now the seat of the *Balearic Islands Parliament*.

From Plaza de Pio XII to Plaza de la Reina runs the *Paseo del Born*, one of the city's most cosmopolitan avenues, which was begun in the 19th century.

The *Church of Saint Francis* was begun in 1281. On the outside it boasts a magnificent Baroque main-front by Francisco de Herrera (17th century) and, inside the church, which consists of the nave, we find the interesting Gothic tomb of Ramon Llull, the Franco-Gothic altar-piece of Saint Ursula (14th century) and the reredos by Maestro de San Francisco (15th century). Adjoining the convent is the beautiful Gothic cloister.

The *Lonja* or ancient Commercial Exchange and Labour Mart was built on the instigation of James I the Conqueror, although work was not begun on it until 1426. La Lonja is currently the home of the Provincial Fine Arts Museum, and contains many major paintings and sculptures.

Next to the Lonja is the *Consulado del Mar* (Maritime Consulate), the former Merchant Shipping Tribunal,

Front of the Town Hall.

Overall view of Bellver Castle.

which is now the seat of the Regional Government of the Balearic Islands.

Linking the Paseo de Sagrera to the vicinity of Porto-Pi runs the *Paseo Marítimo* which winds for 3 km around the lovely bay of Palma, with a wide range of hotels, restaurants, discothèques, etc., amply catering to the needs of the tourist.

Situated on a hill-top, 2 km from the centre of Palma, and 137 m above sea-level, is the *Castillo de Bellver*. The castle, which was the ancient palace and military head-quarters of the kings of Majorca, commands all the approach routes to Palma, by both sea and land. Building on the castle began in 1300, in the days of James II, under the supervision of Pere Salvà. With its unusual circular structure it provides an excellent example of military architecture in the 14th and 15th centuries. The plan of the building consists of several concentric circles with three adjoining round towers.

Particularly noteworthy are the keep; the round courtyard with its ogival galleries; the chapel containing fragments of the wrought iron screen and medieval pottery; the

Partial view of Plaza de España.

View of the S'Hort del Rei Gardens.

cell where Jovellanos was imprisoned, and the Municipal Museum of Palma, which numbers among its treasures a remarkable Roman head and mosaic, ancient coins, period furniture, several pieces of pottery and bronze objects from the Talaiotic Age, and an interesting 18th-century map of the city of Palma.

Palma offers its visitors a wide range of leisure activities, among others the bull ring for fans of the ''corrida'', or the *Plaza Gomila* in El Terreno district for those who enjoy a hectic night life.

◁ *View of the courtyard of Bellver Castle.*

Overall view of El Arenal, on the east coast.

EL ARENAL — CA'N PASTILLA

Palma possesses a natural balcony overlooking the sea which stretches more than 20 km from east to west, from El Arenal to Ca's Català.

The beaches in this area are connected by two major roads — the Paseo Marítimo and the coast road. As we commence our tour of Majorca we should point out that the whole island without exception is characterised by its peace and harmony, and it is rightly known as the "island of tranquillity".

Majorca is a constant revelation to the visitor, its mountains no less beautiful than its coastline, its people overflowing with hospitality, its "cuisine" a delight to even the most refined palate, and its customs capturing the interest of all those who are fascinated by tradition. The "Mare Nostrum", or Mediterranean, plays an extremely important part in the life of the island, and the Majorcans have taken full advantage of it in building up a network of systems and services supporting a huge tourist industry.

All this, added to Majorca's privileged geographical situation, makes the island a major summer resort.

The bay of Palma begins, to the east, at Cap Blanc. In the middle of the bay lies Cala Blava and, continuing along the coast to the east of Palma, we come to the beaches of El Arenal and Ca'n Pastilla.

12 kilometres from Palma, we find the spacious beach of El Arenal which, with its exceptionally fine sand and clean, clear water, provides the tourist with an ideal spot for a family summer holiday, with attractions for people of all ages. El Arenal is currently one of Majorca's most up-to-date and popular tourist resorts. The 4 km which separate Ca'n Pastilla and El Arenal, including Las Maravillas, and which form what is known as *''Playa de Palma''*, are literally packed with hotels, apartments, restaurants, bars, discothèques and shops. This is a tourist area with a busy night life lasting well into the early hours. The beach is one of Majorca's biggest with a leisure harbour at its eastern tip. Before moving on towards Ca'n

Partial view of El Arenal.

Pastilla, it is worth going a few kilometres inland to visit the church of La Porciúncula. It belongs to the Franciscan order, of which two distinguished Majorcans were members — Ramon Llull and Friar Junípero Serra. The church is regarded as one of the most modern works of religious art on the island, and is moreover situated in a natural park of incomparable beauty.

Only 7 km from Palma is the area known as Ca'n Pastilla, one of the longest-established summer resorts within easy reach of the city. Nowadays, because of its proximity to Palma, it has practically become another district of the city, but its lively, busy atmosphere lends it the character of an important town-centre.

Ca'n Pastilla has a large marina with mooring for 500 yachts, only 3 km from Son Sant Joan airport. Ca'n Pastilla beach is at the western tip of Playa de Palma. So, adjoining Palma, in the tiny

El Arenal and Ca'n Pastilla offer the visitor an enormous range of leisure and entertainment amenities.

Partial view of Ca'n Pastilla.

fishing port of Portitxol, we find the beginnings of a large tourist complex which includes Ciudad Jardín and Cala Gamba, and extends as far as Ca'n Pastilla and El Arenal. Everything we could possibly want is to be found in this area; leisure harbours, amusement parks, swimming pools, tennis courts, minigolf, horse-riding etc., and at night a lively, friendly atmosphere in the restaurants, bars and discothèques. Whatever the time of year, every day on Majorca is a holiday and full of fun although, thanks to careful planning, the words of the painter and poet Santiago Rusiñol still hold true: "Dear Reader, (...) if you wish to enjoy the rest deserved by those who have done no harm to any living soul, follow me to an island I know, an island where it is always peaceful, where men never hurry, where women do not show the signs of aging, where nothing — not even words — is wasted, where the sun lingers longest and where even the moon seems more reluctant to take her leave. Dear Reader, that island is Majorca."

FROM CALA MAJOR TO COSTA D'EN BLANES

To reach the west coast of the island, we travel from Palma along the Paseo Marítimo, passing on our way the Club de Mar and a historic monument called the Pelaires Tower, the ancient watchtower of Porto-Pi, dating from the 15th century, which stands in striking contrast to the other modern buildings. Originally, there were two towers defending the old port of Palma, thus allowing the inlet to be chained off and access to the port prevented. When Palma outgrew this dock, a new one was constructed, thereby laying the foundations of the port as it is today. Another of the buildings we shall pass on our way is Marivent Palace, designed by the architect Forteza, which is the summer residence of the Spanish royal family.

Cala Major, on the west coast of Majorca.

Cala Major and environs boast magnificent sports and residential facilities.

Proceeding along this road we find ourselves in a paradise of small coves and magnificent beaches. Perfect harmony reigns between the local vegetation and the modern tourist amenities.

At no time on our tour shall we lose sight of the blue Mediterranean which leads us from one secluded cove to the next, all of them carved out of the rock and sheltered by green pine-woods.

The first one we encounter is *Cala Major*, with its tiny coves nestling at the foot of low cliffs.

Cala Major is one of the most

Ca's Català and Sant Agustí with, in the background, the yacht club Cala Nova.

popular beaches, attracting islanders, visitors from the mainland and from all over the world. It is protected by its strategic position from any extremes of climate which, in any event, are rare in the region around Palma.

As a result of the great influx of tourists, a large complex of hotels, apartments, restaurants, bars, cafeterias and all kinds of shops has grown up in the area surroun-

View of Illetes Beach.

*View of the rocky coast of Ses Illetes
and, in the background, Portals Nous.*

ding Cala Major. There are also a great many discothèques and souvenir shops.

From Cala Major we shall make our way to the village of Gènova to visit the caves. They are small, but very beautiful, and made up of a number of tiny chambers containing reddish and white formations of mineral deposits.

Next to Cala Major there is another busy tourist resort, *Sant Agustí,* with its numerous villas and hotels straddling the hill. It also has a large leisure harbour and sailing school. 7 kilometres away from Palma is *Ca's Català,* the city's own original summer resort.

Nowadays, it is well endowed with modern hotels, sports facilities and entertainments of all kinds.

The tourist can be sure of finding a wide range of activities to occupy his time; parties, competitions, sports, etc.

Beaches we shall come across next on our tour belong to the district of Calvià.

Calvià, which used to be a mainly agricultural area, has now been taken over by the tourist industry, its important tourist amenities

making it highly attractive to the visitor. The residential area lies next to the sea, and is surrounded by the pine trees which are so typical of this region. Because of this, the temperature on these beaches is very agreeable both in winter and in summer.

On this part of the coast we shall visit the estate developments of *Illetes, Portals Nous and Costa d'en Blanes*, with its dolphin park.

Still in the bay of Palma, 2 km away

Popular, lively Illetes Beach.

The Portals Nous Yacht Club.

from Ca's Catala we come to *Illetes*.

Three small rocky islands, floating just offshore in the transparent, sparkling water give this beach its name.

People say that the water here is so clear that the tops of the pine trees reflected in it seem to brush against the bathers as they swim. The area around Illetes has many luxury hotels, elegant restaurants and a multitude of cafes and night-clubs.

The beach at Illetes, though small, is one of the best beaches near Palma.

It is superbly sheltered from inclement weather by pine-clad hills which slope down towards the sea. From Illetes we can take a trip inland to visit the Palace or Castle of Bendinat (Feastwell Castle).

This is a splendid area of gardens and pine-woods, with a palace dating from the middle of the 19th century. It was given this name, people say, because King James I, after eating a frugal meal in this neighbourhood consisting of a loaf

of bread and some garlic, generously exclaimed: "Bé hem dinat!" (What a feast we've had!) Let us now return to the main road where we shall once again be dazzled by the amazing blue of the sea.

We shall proceed westward enjoying the coves which are wonderfully warm in winter and cool in summer.

Cala de Portals Nous.

Partial view of Portals Nous.

Portals Nous is a development which blends perfectly and harmoniously into the landscape, the whole area being overlooked by a lush pine-wood. The rocks have formed a natural pool protected against rough waves. Not far from the sea, there is an oratory which is open to visitors.

The whole area stretching from Cala Major to Costa d'en Blanes has outstanding appeal for the tourist, combining natural beauty with man-made attractions designed to delight the visitor and make his leisure time even more enjoyable.

Magnificent residential areas, restaurants, villas and sports complexes, and an excellent harbour offering exceptional facilities for visitors who wish to drop anchor and enjoy a few days' rest.

All this shows how Majorca, the "island of tranquillity" still maintains that maritime tradition and love of sailing for which the island was famous a few centuries ago.

Night-time view of Palma Nova.

FROM PALMA NOVA — MAGALLUF TO CAMP DE MAR

Palma Nova is a magnificent beach situated 14 km from Palma which delights the visitor with its fine-textured, dazzling warm sand.

All along the modern promenade which follows the curve of the beach there are top-quality hotels and residential complexes. In Torrenova, one apartment block is particularly remarkable for its interesting painted mural, the work of the artists Arranz Bravo and Bartolozzi. Palma Nova, with its wide avenues, and relaxed, cheerful atmosphere, began to develop its coastline around 1960, thus becoming one of the key sites in the spectacular transformation of the island brought about by the tourist boom.

Palma Nova offers a wide selection of fun and entertainments; various types of water sports, an aquapark, horse riding or tennis, or simply whiling away the time on a comfortable deck-chair in the warm sun.

In the evenings, the terraces of the bars along the beach are the ideal spot for sitting and enjoying a view of the incomparable sunsets to be seen here. At night, after savouring a tasty meal in one of the area's excellent restaurants, the visitor can chose between a modern discothèque, a flamenco show or spending a quiet evening having a drink in one of the many cosy pubs. Palma Nova beach is closely followed by that of *Magalluf*, and together they form a tourist complex sheltered by pine trees, which stretches for 5 km along the coast in an unbroken line, save where it is interrupted by the tiny peninsula of Punta de sa Porrassa.

Magalluf has become an exceptional leisure centre thanks to its clear, transparent sea water, the quality of its hotels and apartments, its wide variety of shops, the good service in its bars and restaurants, and to the innumerable forms of entertainment it offers, all of which guarantee that the visitor's stay here will be supremely enjoyable. Nearby, there is an 18-hole golf course, tennis courts, go-kart tracks, gliding, horse riding,

Partial view of Palma Nova.

water skiing and water parachuting, etc..

Also at Magalluf, Majorca's casino provides, in addition to the gaming tables, first-rate service and entertainment by internationally acclaimed performers.

Palma Nova and Magalluf, together with the equally popular *Cala Vinyes*, are the last major tourist haunts on this part of the bay of Palma. However, if we follow the road down towards the west, we shall come to a beautiful, secluded little cove known as *Portals Vells*. Its quiet, relatively uncrowded beach, contrasts with the bustle and activity of the beaches described above and makes it the perfect place for those who wish to get away from the crowd.

In the attractive vicinity of Portals Vells, a path leads us to the entrance of a cave, the *Cova de la Mare de Déu* (the Grotto of the Mother of God) situated in an ancient quarry where, in former times, there stood a much revered

Overall view of the beach at Palma Nova.

Magalluf Beach.

statue of the Virgin. According to scholars, this statue belonged to the Mozarabic community of Majorca during the time of Arab rule; however, according to popular tradition the figure came from a Genoese ship which was threatened by a terrible storm.

Terrified by the impending disaster, the ship's crew vowed that, if they emerged unscathed from the tragedy, they would leave the statue wherever they first came ashore in an act of thanksgiving. Thus, the statue remained in the cave until 1866, when it was

Tiny square, Magalluf.

decided to transfer it to a new chapel which had been erected in Portals Nous, where it can still be seen today.

The cove at Portals Vells, together with the tiny *Cala Figuera* and its lighthouse, marks the end of the eastern tip of the bay of Palma.

From Palma Nova, the road leads through aromatic pine-woods to *Santa Ponça*, still within the district of Calvià, the island's foremost tourist area.

Santa Ponça is an exceptionally

Night-time view of Magalluf.

Cala Vinyes.

beautiful little bay, enjoying a privileged position and sheltered from inclement weather by its rocky coast.

It has a harbour with numerous pleasure boats.

In addition to the undeniable charm of its evocative scenery, Santa Ponça has considerable historic interest, as is witnessed by its many remains and monuments dating from former ages, such as a Gothic turret or watch-tower, which reminds us of the time when coastal raids were commonplace. A cross, called ''Sa Creu del Rei en Jaume'' (King James' Cross), situated at the tip of the promontory which separates the beach from the harbour, commemorates the most important historic event associated with Santa Ponça and one of the most significant for Majorca as a whole; on 10th September, 1229, Catalan-Aragonese troops commanded by King James I the Conqueror disembarked on the beach, ready to free the island from Arab rule. On the base of the monumental cross, which was erected seven centuries later in 1929, various scenes from the exploit are captured in sculpture.

Near the place where the cross was erected, there is a neo-Romanesque chapel designed by Mossèn Alcover i Sureda with sculptures by Tomás Vila. Inside the chapel is the sacred stone which was used as an altar during the first religious ceremony celebrated by the Christian army on Majorcan soil. It is for this reason that the chapel is known as the "Capella de sa Pedra Sagrada" (Chapel of the Sacred Stone).

From Santa Ponça, the Catalan-Aragonese expedition began its conquest of the island. Two days after the landing, there was an important battle against Arab troops at the spot known as "Coll de sa Batalla" (Battle Gorge).

During the course of this battle, the Catalan noblemen Guillem de Montcada, Viscount of Bearn, and Ramon de Montcada, Lord of Tortosa, lost their lives, causing great distress to King James.

In 1887, a cross was erected on this site in memory of the heroism

Another view of Cala Vinyes.

Overall and partial views of Santa Ponça.

of the two brave noblemen on the field of battle.

Santa Ponça and its bay constitute a unique area with every imaginable attraction to guarantee a good holiday. Every year, thousands of visitors are drawn to Santa Ponça by its brilliant blue sea, its green pines and the striking contrast between its impressive cliffs and its tranquil beaches.

Moving on to the vista-point at Malgrat, we shall enjoy the superb view of the bay of Santa Ponça. In the distance, to the right, we can

Two views of the beach at Santa Ponça.

see the outline of Sa Mola Point; in the foreground, we can see the Cap d'es Llamp (Lightning Point) and the beaches of Camp de Mar and Peguera, separated by the promontory of Cap Andritxol. To the left of the vista-point, we can see the small island of El Toro and the cove of Ses Penyes Rotges; directly opposite, against a blue backdrop we can see the islands of Malgrat.

From the top of "Sa Morisca" hill, which is the site of a Bronze Age "talaiot" or megalithic structure,

The Malgrat Isles, opposite the coast at Santa Ponça. ▷

View of the so-called "Costa de la Calma".

we enjoy a clear view of practically all the Calvià area, together with a large section of the coast.

As well as its attractive landscapes, Santa Ponça boasts modern hotels, cafeterias, restaurants, a marina (one of thirty on the island of Majorca), a golf course ...

Situated on the bay of Santa Ponça itself is *Peguera*, an important, cosmopolitan tourist resort which has undergone extraordinary expansion over the last few years. Peguera has become one of the most prosperous areas on Majorca, thanks to the undeniable beauty of its three fine, sandy beaches, the charming pine trees which reach down as far as the water's edge, and mildness of its own particular climate. This tourist spot offers all the entertainments one could wish to find, from one's favourite water sports to excursions using various means of transport, or a lively night life.

For lovers of the past, the area around Peguera has some very interesting historic remains dating from the Bronze Age, such as a group of elongated structures and a "talaiot" which was used for defence purposes.

Only a few minutes away from Peguera, on the road which leads to Andratx, we come to *Cala Fornells*, where a residential village of villas and hotels has grown up at the water's edge.

This beauty spot has a small but very fine, sandy beach, and enjoys some outstandingly beautiful sunsets.

Scarcely two kilometres from Cala Fornells, enclosed between the two headlands, Andritxol and d'es Llamp, we find the secluded beach of *Camp de Mar*, with its white sand and dazzling blue water.

Camp de Mar has many comfortable hotels and residential areas, swimming pools, bars, ... and a distinctive rocky island opposite the beach, linked to it by a small bridge, where the visitor can take refreshment in the bar.

Any of the tourist resorts we have mentioned, whether those situated on the bay of Palma, or those belonging to the southern tip of the west coast, are ideal places to

Overall view of Paguera.

Mallorca

SA CALOBRA ★ Torre
de Pa

PORT DE SÓLLER

SÓLLER
DEIÀ ALFÀBIA

BANYALBUFAR VALLDEMOSSA

Sa Dragonera

PORT
D'ANDRATX

Castell de Bellver ★
CALA MAJOR
PEGUERA PALMA CAN PASTILLA
DE MALLORCA *Aeroport
Son San Ju*
CAMP DE MAR PALMA NOVA
SANTA PONÇA MAGALLUF S'ARENAL

N

S'EST
CALA PI

SANT VICENÇ

FORMENTOR

POLLENÇA PORT DE POLLENÇA
ALCÚDIA

PORT D'ALCÚDIA

nestir
Lluc

CAN PICAFORT

CALA RATJADA

CAPDEPERA

CALA BONA
CALA MILLOR

SA COMA

S'ILLOT

MANACOR

Coves dels Hams ★

PORTOCRISTO

PORRERES

Coves del Drac

FELANITX

CALA MURADA

UCMAJOR

CAMPOS

PORTO COLOM

SA RÀPITA SANTANYÍ

CALA D'OR
PORTO PETRO

RENC

COLÒNIA DE SANT JORDI

View of Cala Fornells.

Partial view of the picturesque Cala Fornells resort.

spend a wonderful holiday, both because of their natural setting and the wide range of services and amenities they offer, so satisfying the requirements of even the most discerning of visitors.

Leaving Camp de Mar via the road which leads to the port of Andratx, we enjoy an impressive view of the high, rocky coast lined with pine trees, with easy access to the quiet coves below.

Partial view of Andraitx. ▷

FROM ANDRAITX TO BANYALBUFAR

Passing on our left Puig de Son Orlandis and its hermitage, we come to *Port d'Andratx*, whose long quay is overlooked by Sa Mola promontory, and is set in a long, narrow inlet.

On the Mola itself, enduring the passage of time, remains one of the watch towers built in the 16th century to warn the local people of the pirate raids to which the island was subject. From the 15th to the 17th century, this section of the coast

Reminders of the past: galleys and typical Majorcan objects.

Aerial view of the port at Andraitx.

was under constant threat of raids by Arab pirates, which explains why we shall come across several towers of its kind, for example those of Son Mas, Son Esteve, Sant Tem, etc., in this area.

To return to Sa Mola, we should point out that nowadays, it is an exclusive area and a spot favoured by well-known personalities from the world of politics, art, literature, the aristocracy, etc. The history of Port d'Andratx, like that of Majorca's coast as a whole, is closely associated with the traditions of sailing and emigration. The people of Andratx in particular have, for as long as can be remembered, chosen the sea as a means of communication, since it provided the easiest route to Palma.

Port d'Andratx is now full of fishing-boats and yachts bobbing on the water, adding to the picturesque character of this unique spot on the Majorcan coast.

In the vicinity of the harbour there are numerous restaurants, modern residential areas and splendid hotels.

Very near the harbour we find the town of Andratx itself, sheltering in

General view of Sant Elm.

a beautiful valley which is bounded to the north by Estellencs, to the east by Capdellà and Calvià, and to the south-west by the Mediterranean.

The origins of Andratx are uncertain. Some say it is Roman in origin, while others claim that it was founded by Christians fleeing from Turkish pirates. Whatever its true origins, today Andratx is a modern town whose main source of income is its tourist industry, vouchsafed by the beauty of its surroundings.

From Andratx we can take a trip to *Sant Tem*, where we shall see the island of *Sa Dragonera* stretched out in the water like a lizard basking in the sun. In Sant Tem we shall find a 16th-century defence tower and fortified house known as Sa Torre. Sant Tem also has a beach with modern hotels, bars and restaurants.

As we proceed along the road to Estellencs, we shall take the opportunity to pause at successive vistapoints on the way, such as *Ricardo Roca*, on the Grao tunnel itself, from which we can admire the Mediterranean in all its immensity.

On approaching *Estellencs* we shall be surprised by the olive, apricot and almond trees growing all around. Estellencs is a small town perched on the mountain-side, rising above an exquisite little cove. Heading towards Banyalbufar, we must stop to visit the *Talaia de Ses Ànimes*, one of Majorca's most ancient watch-towers, from which one of the most impressive views of the island is to be had. Its very name, *Banyalbufar*, which in Arabic means ''little vineyard by the sea'', is an indication of the lush garden that awaits us. Moreover, the town also possesses the famous 15th-century tower ''la Baronia'' and a crystal clear cove.

Now let us take a short trip inland to *La Granja*, near Esporles, one of the most representative mansions to be built in the rural Majorcan style of architecture.

The "Ses Animes" tower.

Overall view of Banyalbufar.

VALLDEMOSSA — SOLLER — TORRENT DE PAREIS

The charming village of *Valldemossa*, which stands at a height of 400 m, is surrounded by mountains, and is famous for its distinguished visitors, including Chopin, George Sand, Archduke Louis Salvatore of Austria, Santiago Rusiñol, Unamuno, Azorín, Rubén Darío, etc.

The best known monument in Valldemossa is the Royal Carthusian Monastery of Jesus of Nazareth, ''Sa Cartoixa'', although the monks were forced to abandon the monastery in 1836 as a result of the Dispossession Act.

The French novelist George Sand and the Polish composer Frédéric Chopin stayed there during the winter of 1838-39. Chopin composed some of his best preludes and nocturnes in Valldemossa, whilst his lover wrote there a book entitled ''Un hiver à Majorque'' (A Winter in Majorca), in which she described the landscape around Valldemossa in the following words: ''Never have I seen a place so delightful and at the same time

The Cartuja (Carthusian Monastery):
library and Chopin's piano.

The wild landscape of Sa Foradada.

so melancholy as this, where the green oak, the carob tree, the pine tree, the olive, the poplar and the cypress mingle their varied hues in a dense, leafy tangle of branches, forming deep green chasms, seared by a rushing torrent beneath a sumptuous undergrowth of exquisite beauty. I shall never forget the spot from which, as one looked back, one could see perched at the top of the hill one of those lovely little Moorish houses, (...) half hidden amongst the folliage of the walnut trees, and the silhouette of a tall palm tree bending over into the void. When I'm plunged into ennui by the sight of the mud and fog of Paris, I close my eyes and see once more, as in a dream, that verdant mountain, those bare rocks, and that solitary palm tree outlined against a distant, rose-coloured sky.''

Building on the monastery began in 1399 on the same sight as the old Arab *vali* palace and that of the kings of Majorca. The monastery was given to the Carthusian monks of Scala Dei by King Martin the

One of the age-old olives trees which grow on the island.

Humane. The building was renovated in the 16th, 17th and 18th centuries.

The cell in which Chopin and Georges Sand acted out their stormy love affair has been left almost untouched.

Inside the monastery, the old pharmacy, looking much as it did when the monastery was abandoned by the monks, is of particular interest. The collection of Majorcan xylographs and the cell devoted to the memory of Archduke Louis

Partial view of Cala de Deià.

Overall view of Sóller port.

Salvatore — the Austrian aristocrat writer and scientist who spent many years on the island — are also of interest. The Archduke arrived on Majorca in 1867 under the assumed title of Count Neudorf.

Inside the church of the Carthusian monastery, which is Neoclassical in style and built on the plan of a Roman cross, there are several interesting frescoes by Friar Miguel Bayeu, two paintings by Friar Joaquín Juncosa, a Virgin of the Sorrows, and a crucifix by the Catalan sculptor Adrià Ferran, sacred ornaments, and various pieces of marquetry.

The house where Saint Catherine Thomas was born is next to the parish church, and was converted into an oratory in 1792.

Another monument worth visiting is the Palace of King Sancho, with its outstanding defence tower. It is a luxurious, tastefully furnished mansion which provides an ideal setting for folk exhibitions.

On a hillside near Valldemossa, in a strikingly beautiful place, stands the Hermitage of the Trinity. It was

Partial view of the port at Sóller.

founded in 1648, although the present buildings date from 1703.

So stunning and breathtakingly spectacular is the landscape around Valldemossa, that the visitor is spellbound in admiration of it. There are many lay-byes along the corniche from which to contemplate this unique panorama, with its impressive blue sea. It is quite simple "out of this world".

Son Moragues is a stately home with a fine gallery and inner courtyard.

The charming tram which links Sóller with its port.

Aerial view of Torrent de Pareis.

In 1276, Ramon Llull founded on this estate a school of Oriental languages under the sponsorship of King James II and with the approval of Pope John XXI. It was the first missionary school ever to be created in Christendom.

In 1485, Nicolau Calafat of Valldemossa printed a book at "Trinitat de Valldemossa", that is to say, *Miramar,* on the first Majorcan printing-press.

When Archduke Louis Salvatore of Austria arrived on the island in the last century, he was captivated by its beauty. The experience of ex-

Partial view of Sa Calobra.

ploring and discovering the island was of major importance in his life. His activities here commenced when he acquired a small estate called Miramar. This was only the beginning of his extensive properties on Majorca, which he built up out of a desire to protect the flora and fauna of the island.

He purchased Son Galceran, Son Gallart, Son Ferrandell and Son Moragues, followed some time later by Son Marroig and Son Gual. It was at Miramar that he wrote his ambitious encyclopaedia ''Die Balearen'' (The Balearic Isles) in German. Towards the end of the 19th century, he had a chapel built on a rock in the shape of a rotunda, containing a statue of Ramon Llull.

At *Son Marroig*, in the district of Deià, there is a museum devoted to the Archduke, with belvederes commissioned by the Archduke himself; one of these contains an Ionic pavilion built of Carrara marble; the other looks out onto

The "nudo de la corbata" ("Tie knot") on the road to Sa Calobra.

Mouth of the Pareis.

''Sa Foradada'', one of nature's own extravaganzas, with its headland in the shape of a dolphin's head, and its majestic view.

The village of *Deià* is surrounded by wonderful scenery, its stone houses nestling in a valley, and its steep streets lined with well-tended gardens.

The English writer Robert Graves lived in Deià for many years. Many other writers and artists have made this charming villaage their home. Deià has a lovely cove, and its small beach, although not sandy, is bathed by beautifully clean water.

On our way to Sóller, we shall pass through Lluc-Alcari, a small village with typical houses and crystal-clear water.

Sóller is a fine small town, 10 km from Deià and is the chief town of one Majorca's most important districts.

The town has an unusual layout, its streets and sturdy houses arranged around the main square.

Of special interest are the Mordernist-style (Art Nouveau-inspired) parish church, which was the work of the architect Juan Rubió, and the 18th-century houses which give the town an aristocratic air. This lovely town and its valley are surrounded by high mountains.

Sóller is linked to its charming harbour by a picturesque old tram-car. From Sóller we can take a trip to *Alfàbia*, where we shall find a large stately home of Arab origin with lovely gardens, or we can take the road known as Coll de Sóller, which will give us an impressive view of *Puig Major*, the highest peak on the island, rising out of the fertile valley of Sóller.

View of the beach at Torrent de Pareis, and a view of the wild countryside.

Overall view of the Lluc monastery.

To reach Sa Calobra and Torrent de Pareis, we shall descend by a narrow, twisting road along a section known as "the tie-knot".

Sa Calobra is beside the Torrent de Pareis, and has a boarding-house and restaurant, and a small beach. There is a path leading to the torrent's outlet, and whose final section of about 200 m is a narrow tunnel.

The *Torrent de Pareis* flows for 4 km, and finally opens into the sea. Its course has carved out a deep gully whose depth varies between 300 and 400 metres. The landscape is dramatic, with a wild kind of beauty. One of its hidden crannies, called Sa Fosca, never sees the light of day.

The landscape at the mouth of the stream is astonishingly beautiful, where the torrent joins the sea between two colossal bare rocks.

At the point where the Torrent de Pareis flows into the sea, there is a beach.

From Sa Calobra and Torrent de Pareis, those two uniquely lovely spots painted by the Catalan artist Joaquim Mir and others, we move on to Escorca, the district in which we find the famous *Sanctuary of Lluc*.

This is the major shrine on Majorca, situated 25 km from Pollença. Here the Virgin of Lluc, "La Moreneta" the Patron Saint of Majorca is venerated. The Monastery of Lluc was originally built in the Gothic style, although the present building dates from the 17th century.

There is an interesting treasure gallery containing archaeological finds, objects related to monastery life, and valuable works of art. In one of the rooms there is a folk museum with one of the island's best collections of Majorcan pottery.

The monastery has a hostel for pilgrims. It also has a number of rooms occupied by the "Blauets", the children who go to school there and form the monastery choir.

POLLENÇA AND FORMENTOR

Before continuing on our journey along the Majorcan coast, it would

Environs of the Lluc monastery: the rock known as the Camel.

View of Cala Sant Vicenç.

be interesting to travel inland and visit *Inca*, the third most important city on the island.

Among its monuments, the church of Santa María la Mayor is particularly eye-catching. It was originally Gothic, but was practically reconstructed in the early 18th century in the Baroque style. Of the original church only the 13th-century bell tower remains. Also within the town, the convents of Saint Dominic and Saint Francis, both with 18th-century cloisters, are of interest.

About 5 km from the town, on the Puig d'Inca, stands the hermitage of Saint Magdelene. It commands one of the most beautiful panoramas of the island.

Inca has a long tradition of artisan shoe manufacturing which, with the passage of time, has become an important and famous industry, now expanded to include the manufacture of suede and leather clothes.

Also in a state of good conservation are some ''cellers'' used for storing wine in the 19th century; nowadays they serve as restaurants offering typical Major-

Monument to the painter Llorenç Cerdà.

can cuisine, and retaining their original interior decoration, including wine presses and barrels. Every Thursday there is a bustling market in the town held in the square in front of the Town Hall and spilling over into adjoining streets. This motley market attracts a large number of visitors. On the way to Pollença, 37 km from Palma, we find the *Campanet Caves*. These caves run underground for 1,300 m and approximately half of them are no

Partial view of Cala Sant Vicenç.

Overall view of Pollença.

longer subject to the effects of water. Thus, in some of the caves, there are large mineral formations, whilst in others there are delicate stalactites, depending on the position of the cave.

Just before Pollença, on the right, a 333-metre high mountain called ''Puig'' rears its head. On its summit stands a 13th-century oratory which was originally used by the Poor Clares and later by hermits. Inside the oratory, there is an interesting collection of votive

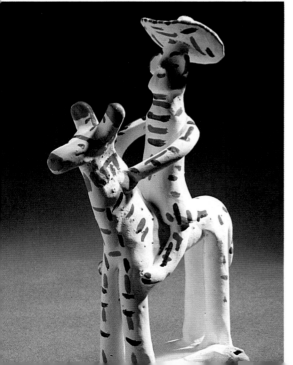

The typical Majorcan whistle known as the siurell, *in the form of a clay figure. Its origins is thought to go back to the time of the Phoenicians.*

offerings. Alongside, there is a guest-house.

Pollença, framed in a beautiful landscape, is a small town with a considerable artistic heritage. Among its many monuments the following are of special interest: the parish church with its high tower; the austere convent of Saint Dominic, within whose cloisters the International Music Festival is held in the month of August and which draws renowned soloists and conductors; and the church of Montesion and the Gothic oratory of Roser Vell.

The layout of Pollença is very attractive with its winding streets — Miquel Costa i Llobera, the Majorcan poet, was born in the street that bears his name; its russet houses and delightful fountains, some of them very famous, such as "Font del Gall".

Next to the town is a little hill called "Calvari" (Calvary), with a flight of 365 steps leading to the top, and which may also be reached by a pathway which runs up the hill. At the top there is an oratory where the Crucified Christ and the "Verge

The Roman bridge at Pollença.

Overall view and detail of the port at Pollença.

del Peu de la Creu'' (Virgin of the Foot of the Cross) are venerated. The view from the vista-point is spectacular.

Cala de Sant Vicenç belongs to Pollença, and is situated about 7 km to the north of the town. It is a singularly beautiful cove, divided into small beaches with fine white sand, bounded on the east by inaccessible cliffs, and on the south by a huge pine-wood. The cove, which has excellent facilities for the summer, lies at the head of the promontory of Formentor at the northernmost tip of the island.

Port de Pollença an old haven for fishermen, has become a splendid tourist resort. This is where the Anglada Camarasa Museum, housing a good collection of the artist's paintings and drawings is to be found.

The countryside between Port de Pollença and Formentor is truly marvellous, indeed it is unforgettable. The vista-point at Es Colomer, overlooking the port and the bay, commands beautiful panoramas.

The well-known Hotel Formentor, where the first international "Formentor Novel Award" was celebrated stands in the cove called Pi de la Posada. The hotel, inaugurated in 1931 by Adan Diehl, has since played host to such internationally acclaimed personalities as the Prince and Princess of Monaco and the Duke and Duchess of Kent.

At the foot of the hotel lies the fine sandy beach, the blue sea and luxuriant pines, presided over by a tiny

The Formentor road and Es Colomer.

Cala Figuera (Formentor).

island. The beauty of Formentor was sung in verses of the Majorcan poet Costa i Llobera, in whose honour a monument was erected at nearby Cala Murta. From the lighthouse of Formentor, the ever-changing vistas are of an indescribable beauty.

Indeed, the entire peninsula of *Formentor* can be considered one of the most scenic spots on Majorca.

The Xara Gate in the old city walls of Alcúdia.

ALCÚDIA AND CAN PICAFORT

Little more than 9 km from Pollença harbour lies *Alcúdia*, at the northern tip of the bay to which it gives its name. A road runs from the small town to the northern side of the Victoria peninsula, which ends at Cap d'es Pinar. This is where the summer resorts Mal Pas and Bon Aire are to be found. The road hugs the coastline, winding its way through pine-woods, until it reaches the hermitage at La Vic-toria, which was built in the 13th century and rebuilt in the 17th century. It contains a Gothic carved wooden statue of the Virgin, who is Patroness of the town.

The walled city of Alcúdia is very near the ancient Roman city of *Pollentia*. Once a flourishing centre, today, this quiet peaceful town welcomes the visitor to a wealth of interesting monuments which bear witness tom its illustrious past. Its origins can be traced back to the days when it wass recolonised

View of the port of Alcúdia.

after the island's conquest by James I.

James II of Majorca gave it the status of a municipality in 1298. In 1362, the first city walls of Alcúdia were finished, later to be extended and rebuilt in the 16th century. The Gate of Majorca, otherwise called the Gate of Saint Sebastian and the Gate of Xara or the Port Gate, still stand to this day, whilst the remainder of the wall has been recently rebuilt.

Most outstanding of the city's monuments are the 13th-century chapel of Saint Anne and the 19th-century parish church which replaced the earlier church which was destroyed and of which only the Renaissance chapel of the Holy Christ remains unscathed.

Housed in the Archaeological Centre are valuable bronze and marble statues, ceramics and gravestones which were rescued from the ruins of Pollentia, the city founded by the Romans in the 1st century B.C., and which was pillaged and burnt in the 4th century. On the road to Port de Alcúdia, we shall see the ancient Roman theatre whose harmonious proportions are readily appreciated.

Port d'Alcúdia, 3 km from the town, is one of the most sheltered spots on the bay and is now not only an important tourist resort but also a key commercial centre.

Between this point and the Farrutx promontory stretch 15 km of beaches curving round the bay.

Two developments, those of Lago Menor and Lago Mayor, which together form the so-called "Ciudad de los Lagos" are right next to the sea.

"Albufera de Mallorca" is Majorca's first and only natural park which has been open since 1988. It is a humid and rich bird sanctuary frequented by mainly migratory birds.

Can Picafort is a lively tourist area with a pleasant white sandy beach.

Partial view of Cala Ratjada.

Artà.

ARTA — CAPDEPERA — CALA RATJADA

Capdepera is an inland small town whose nearby coast is an important tourist resort. Its castle, a walled medieval fortress, stands intact. The road which runs round it command a broad view of the coast. 3 km from Capdepera is *Cala Ratjada*, a beautiful fishing port which has now become a popular holiday centre.

The whole coast is dotted with coves and alternating beaches overlooked by pine-woods, such as Cala Agulla or Son Moll.

Heading inland once again we come to *Artà*, with its elegant, stately mansions and, close to the town centre, the magnificent ''talaiotic'' settlement of Ses Països, thought to be one of the best preserved set of megalithic structures, and which has been listed as a Historical-Artistic monument.

Near Cala Ratjada, in the district of Capdepera, are the famous *Caves of Artà*, with their strangely

The Ses Païses Talayot settlement at Artà.

beautiful stalactites and stalagmites.

The gaping entrance to the caves is situated on the edge of a cliff 46 m above sea level. Of its numerous chambers, the Hall of Columns, the Fairy Grotto and the Hall of Flags are particularly interesting.

Canyamel is an agreeable beach of the whitest sand. Moving inland we come across Torre de Canyamel, a magnificent 13th-century tower.

Entrance to the Artà caves.

The beach at Canyamel.

COSTA DE LOS PINOS AND SON SERVERA BAY

As we continue on our journey along the east coast of the island, we come to a new bay, Son Servera Bay which stretches from the Pinar promontory to Punta de N'Amer.

The road that runs parallel to the coast has various turn-offs leading to modern developments, quiet coves and beaches of fine white sand, such as Costa de los Pinos, Port Vell, Port Nou, Cala Bona and Cala Millor.

Costa de los Pinos is the tourist centre at the top of Son Servera bay and constitutes one of the loveliest spots on Majorca.

Port Vell is a tiny fishing port which has also become a select residential area. It has a nine-hole golf course.

We shall take the turning that leads inland to *Son Servera*.

Son Servera was traditionally an agricultural small town, but recently it has experienced a great economic boom thanks to the development of the tourist industry along its coast.

It has an interesting and perfectly conserved medieval tower adjoining the parish church which was a chapel in the 17th century.

Another road will bring us back to the coast, to *Cala Bona* which has a leisure harbour.

Cala Millor offers a wide range of

Aerial view of Canyamel and a view of the Costa de los Pinos.

Aerial view of Cala Millor.

amenities for pursuing all kinds of sports, from diving to underwater fishing, or tennis for which it is equipped with numerous courts. All of the tourist resorts on the bay have a lively night life, with good restaurants, terraced cafes and cosmopolitan discothèques. Close to Punta de N'Amer, a reproduction of an African safari park has been created that can be visited by car.

S'Illot. Sa Coma. Cala Millor. Cala Bona.

Sa Coma Beach.

PORTO CRISTO — MANACOR CAVES

From Punta de N'Amer onwards, the sea takes on a specially vivid blue and the beaches and coves continue to impress their beauty upon the visitor: *Playa de Sa Coma, Cala Moreia, S'Illot, Cala Morlanda...*

In olden days, most of these beaches and coves were a haven for pirates, and when this danger ceased to exist, they became a gateway to the sea for the small villages round about.

With the passage of time, the attractive landscapes made this part of the coast a favourite summer resort for people living in nearby villages.

Today, Majorcan holiday-makers share the peace and beauty of this landscape with tourists from other parts of the world. Besides its delightful scenery, this part of the coast has attractions for people of all ages and has facilities for underwater fishing. If we temporarily leave the coast to travel inland, we shall come to the second most important city in the Balearic archipelago: *Manacor*, 13 km from the coast. Manacor is an agricultural town which also has a thriving industry. Manacor has two important industries: carpentry and imitation pearls.

The furniture manufacturing industry is so well established that as far back as the 17th century, carpenters in the town formed their own guild, breaking away from the one in Palma. The first furniture factory there as such goes back to 1860.

Various commercial centres in the city display fine wooden objects carefully manufactured and of a very high quality.

The imitation pearl industry in Manacor is the other typical activity of the town and one that has made it internationally famous. Besides admiring the beautiful jewellery made from these wonderful pearls, we can also visit some of its factories.

In the city we can admire the Gothic parish church although it

Night-time view of Porto Cristo.

Overall view of Porto Cristo.

underwent neo-Gothic renovation in the 19th century. From the bell tower we enjoy the marvellous view of the plain of Manacor and the coast.

Also of interest are the Baroque cloisters of the convent of Saint Dominic, the 14th-century Torre de Ses Puntes, with its collection of mosaics, the Miniature Furniture Museum, containing interesting miniatures of antique furniture from Majorca and other parts of Spain, the Municipal Museum of Archaeology with *talaiotic*, Roman and Paleochristian pieces. The latter are from the Byzantine basilicas of Sa Carrotja and Son Peretó, etc. The *Cuevas dels Hams* are on the road from Manacor to Porto Cristo. They were discovered in 1906, although they only recently opened to the public.

Their name "Hams" (fish-hook) is due to the peculiar shape of their delicate white stalactites.

Mention must be made of the underground lake called "Sea of Venice", that can be crossed by boat, as also the "Rest Room" and

*Els Hams Caves.
the Sea of Venice.*

*El Drac Caves.
Martel Lake.*

Aerial view of Punta Reina.

the so-called "Imperial Palace".
Porto Cristo, Manacor's harbour, is one of Majorca's liveliest tourist centres, because of the beauty of the surrounding area, its splendid beach and the nearby Cuevas del Drac. Porto Cristo is one of the oldest anchorages on the island, as was proved by a Roman craft which was found buried in the sand near the shore.

In the Middle Ages, Porto Cristo was a fishing port situated at the innermost point of the narrow, pro-tected inlet. Even today, that old fishing-port atmosphere remains in harmonious coexistence with the world of commerce and tourism.

A visit to the nearby aquarium is well worthwhile.

The *Cuevas del Drac* were explored in 1896 by the French potholer, Edouard Martel, sponsored by Louis Salvatore, Archduke of Austria.

In the words of Martel, the caves formed due to the action of sea water as it seeped through the gaps and cracks in the limestone. The Cuevas del Drac cover an area of about 2 km and consist of four caves: the cave of the French, Louis Salvatore's cave, the white cave and the black cave.

The stalactites and stalagmites which abound in these caves, sometimes in isolation, sometimes together and meeting halfway to fuse in extravagant forms which have been given fanciful names such as "Fairy Theatre" or "Diana's Bath".

The colour of the caves, initially white, takes on reddish or bluish shades depending on natural reflections or the effects of artificial lighting devised by the Catalan engineer Carlos Buigas.

Without the shadow of a doubt, the greatest marvel of the Cuevas del Drac is its Great Lake, commonly known as Martel's lake. It is 177

Cala Romántica.

Partial view of Cala Domingos.

metres long and is thought to be one of the largest underground lakes in the world.

From a boat on the lake, a small orchestra bids the visitor farewell with a recital of classical music which is synchronised with a light show.

Between Porto Cristo and Porto Colon there are innumerable small beaches esconced in some twenty beautiful coves. The so-called *Calas de Mallorca* declared to be of tourist interest because of their exceptional beauty, deserve special mention.

Calas de Mallorca include such exquisite spots as Cala Bota, Cala Soldat, Cala Antena, Cala Domingos and Cala Murada.

Cala Murada belongs to the municipality of Felanitx. It has become a popular summer resort with an expanding urban area. The unusual circular and radial layout of the streets is interesting.

FROM PORTO COLOM TO CALA SANTANYÍ

The small town of *Felanitx*, 12 km from the coast, sits in the shadow of the Sant Salvador massif. Besides producing excellent wine, Felanitx manufactures interesting pottery and has a cooked and cured pork industry.

Well worth noting in the town are the parish church which was begun in the middle of the 14th century and finished at the beginning of the 17th century; the 17th-century convent of Saint Augustin, and some architecturally interesting private houses.

In the vicinity of Felanitx, lying off the road that leads to Porto Colom, is the Puig de Sant Salvador, 509 m high and with a sanctuary and hostel at its summit.

The sanctuary has objects of great artistic value, such as the 14th-century statue of the Virgin and a magnificent stone altar-piece depicting scenes from the Passion.

Overall view of Porto Colom.

View of Cala Ferrera.

From the summit there is a magnificent panoramic view of the coast with Porto Colom in the middle, and on clear days we can see as far as the island of Cabrera. Very close to the sanctuary of Sant Salvador is the Castillo de Santueri, which was formerly an Arab fortress whose earliest origins were perhaps Roman.

A medieval dance called "els cavallets" (the stallions) is still performed in Felanitx. The local festival is celebrated towards the end of August. Open air celebrations at that time are very lively, with people flocking to them over several days.

Porto Colom is a highly attractive fishing port which played an important part in the wine trade at the end of the 19th century. It is full of both fishing-boats and yachts, as well as other pleasure boats.

Porto Colom has many coves lined with pine trees which are the ideal place for wind surfers to practise their favourite sport. At night, the

Partial view of Cala Ferrera.

bars and discothèques teem with life. Further south there are more beaches and coves of great beauty, such as Cala Marçal, Cala Ferrera, Cala Gran, Cala d'Or, Cala Llonga, Cala de ses Egos ...
Cala d'Or is situated 11 km from Porto Colom. It is one of the most beautiful and famous of all Majorca's coves.
Pine-woods line this inlet which, like an estuary, cuts into the coast as far as a small beach with fine sand.

Overall view of Cala Gran.

Porto Cari.

In Cala d'Or there is a development which has been carefully integrated into the landscape. Its houses are white and built in the Ibizan style, shaped like cubes which scale the surrounding hills.

Cala d'Or has modern, comfortable hotels, magnificent recreational facilities and shopping centres.

Near Cala d'Or is *Porto Petro*, another small and picturesque natural port which retains its charming fishing tradition.

Great care has been taken in Porto Petro to ensure that the villas and residential areas built around it blend in perfectly with the village's lovely natural surroundings.

The district of Santanyí on the southern part of the east coast, has approximately 40 km of coastline. It includes Cala d'Or, Porto Petro, Cala Mondragó, Cala Figuera, Cala Santanyí and Cala Llombards. These rugged, craggy coves with their limpid waters and pleasant walks, are ideal spots for bathing. Up to date tourist complexes have sprung up in the surrounding area. *Cala Figuera*, a beautifully long and

Overall view of Cala Figuera.

narrow cove, reminds one of an estuary, as if the sea were stretching out her arms to embrace the land.

Just as in Porto Petro, Cala Figuera achieves a harmonious balance between the colourful atmosphere of its tiny fishing port and the modern comforts of a large tourist centre: villas, hotels, bars, cafeterias, places of entertainment...

The village of *Santanyí* lies about 5 km inland. Its proximity to the coast made it necessary to construct fortifications in order to protect its inhabitants from sea borne attacks. Of the old city walls, construction of which was finished in 1571, only the so called ''Porta Murada'' remains.

Of special interest is the parish church, built of the famous ''pedra de Santanyí'' (Santanyí stone). This stone is very beautiful and has been used in the building of the island's most important architectural monuments, such as Bellver Castle. The parish church houses the famous Rococo organ which originally came from the Convent of Saint Dominic in the city of Palma.

Adjoining the church is a beautiful, old, 14th-century chapel, known as the "Roser", and which was formerly used as the parish church. Close to the village is a hill called Consolación, on whose summit is perched a rustic, old hermitage.

Cala Santanyí, framed in a rugged landscape, has an extensive sandy beach and transparent, limpid waters.

Further south, an imposing rock called Es Pontàs emerges from the sea to form a natural bridge opposite the charming *Cala Llombards*, which also forms part of this rocky landscape.

Cala Llombards is the ideal place to enjoy both sun and sea.

Es Pontàs, near Cala Santanyí and Cala Llombards.

View of Cala Santanyí.

COLONIA DE SANT JORDI

Finally back on the road to Palma, we come to *Ses Salines*, a stop- off for birds of passage. The district contains the Roman cemetery of Sa Carrotja with its tombs hewn out of the rock.

The *Colonia de Sant Jordi* is one of Majorca's best preserved fishing villages. Nearby is the famous ''Platja d'es Trenc'', the last of Majorca's virgin beaches.

Cala Ses Egos.